THE **KOOL** KIDS & THE LAND OF THE **GIANTS**

The Kool Kids and the Land of the Giants
©2017 by James Tate. All rights reserved.

Published by Beyond W8 Loss, LLC, in the United States of America.

ISBN 13: 978-0-9991315-0-3
ISBN 10: 0-9991315-0-8

Illustration: Jay Reed
Interior Design: Brandi K. Etheredge
Copy Editor: Yvette R. Blair-Lavallais

Acknowledgements

Dedicated to my beautiful wife, Triva, and my Kool Kids: Jaxson, Josiah, Justice, and my kool niece, Jenesis. I love you very much.

To the Kool Kids all over the world. Continue to show people that it's kool to be holy and healthy.

It was a nice weekend morning in The Land. Jax & JoJo were looking at themselves in the mirror, admiring the crosses that their dad gave to them. They really liked them.

"Wow! These are really nice crosses," said Jax & JoJo.

"Daddy said it has special powers," said Jax. "I wonder what kind of powers?" asked JoJo.

The brothers went downstairs
where their parents were
making a healthy breakfast
for them.

"Thank you for feeding us
healthy food, Daddy and Mommy,"
said the brothers.

"This food will help us to grow
healthy and strong, right?" asked Jax.

"Yes it will," replied Daddy.
"Eating right, drinking water,
and exercising will keep you both
healthy and strong."

"And don't forget to pray,"
added Mommy.

The boys finished their breakfast.

"Can we go outside please?"
asked Jax.

"Sure, have fun," said Daddy
and Mommy.

Jax and JoJo went outside and
they saw their cousin Jen.
Jen also has a cross necklace that
was given to her by her parents.
Jax, JoJo, and Jen are cousins,
but they are more like siblings.

As they played, a sudden darkness came over The Land. The sudden darkness caused Daddy and Mommy to call the kids into the house.

Daddy turned on the news to see if there was a report about the sudden darkness.

A breaking news report came
over the TV.

"Breaking news! Breaking news!
There has been a giant sighting!
That sudden darkness is the giant's
shadow. We aren't sure what
kind of giant this is, but please
be careful."

"Oh no!" said the kids.

"Daddy, what's a giant?" asked Jax.

Being kids, they never encountered
a giant before.

"Do you remember the story of David
and Goliath? asked Daddy.

"Yes," replied the kids.

"This giant that is in The Land now, is
similar to Goliath. He is here to
terrorize and hurt the people of
The Land," explained Daddy.

The giant has been in The Land for a while now wreaking havoc. The kids have been watching everything from the window in Jax's room. They notice that the people of The Land have grown in size. It seems like the people of The Land are always eating, and the food that they are eating is not good for them.

BREAKING NEWS
THE GIANT'S NAME IS OBESITY!

Another breaking news alert
comes across the TV.

"Breaking News! Breaking News!
The giant has identified himself!
His name is Obesity and he has
issued a statement saying
he is not leaving!"

He has taken many prisoners
and he is looking for more. He
is here forever unless someone
can defeat him!

Many days pass by and no one challenges the giant. The kids look at each other and say...

"We have to do something! This giant can't stay here. He is hurting too many people."

The kids sat down and thought about what to do. Jen says to Jax and JoJo, "You remember what Proverbs 3:5-6 says right?"

"Yes," said the brothers. "It says, Trust in the Lord with all your heart, and lean not on your own understanding. In all your ways acknowledge Him and He will direct your path."

"Exactly!" says Jen. "We should pray and ask God what we should do.

"Right!" said JoJo. "This giant has to go!"

The kids start to pray. As they pray, the crosses around their necks begin to light up.

Two Angels appeared to them
and said, "Hello Kool Kids!"

They looked at each other and asked,
"Did they just call us Kool Kids?"

The Angels continued, "God sent us
to tell you that He loves you and
He hears all of your prayers. Go out
and challenge that giant! We will be
with you. That Cross you wear will
protect you. It will turn into exactly
what you need at the right time."

"Remember, we are always with you,
even if you cannot see us," said
the Angels.

The kids began a transformation process. Their outfits changed and their crosses were different. The Kool Kids are amazed at their new outfits and crosses.

"WOW!!!" said the kids.

"We look like super heroes!" said JoJo.

"Let's go find and defeat Obesity!" said Jax.

"With God and His Angels with us, we can't lose!" said Jen.

Just then, Daddy came
back into the house.
He went out to speak to the
people of The Land about how
they can protect themselves
from Obesity, but no one
wanted to listen. This made
Daddy very sad.

"It's ok Daddy.
Don't be sad!" said Jax.

"Look!!!" all the kids yelled.

The kids showed off their
outfits and new crosses.

Daddy was very happy.

"I see you all prayed for help. Great job!" said Daddy. "You all look kool!"

"I can't wait to see what we can do with our new outfits," said Jen.

"With God on our side, we are going to face Obesity," said Jax.

"And with God, we can't lose," said JoJo.

Daddy prayed over them. "Now, be careful Kool Kids."

Jax, JoJo, and Jen looked at each other.

"I'm really starting to like that name!" they all said at the same time.

"Before you go, I want you to remember the 8 things that people need to do for better health," said Daddy.

"We remember," said the Kool Kids.

"Pray, eat right, pray, drink water, pray, exercise, pray, rest!" said the Kids.

"We must pray before we do anything in life, right Daddy?" asked Jax.

"That's right," replied Daddy.

The Kool Kids picked up their backpacks full of water and healthy snacks and went out on their journey to find Obesity.

On their journey, they noticed how big, sick, and sluggish the people of The Land have become.

"Wow! Obesity sure does a lot of damage to people when he comes," said Jen.

"I see," said Jax.

"This is why he must go! And if no one wants to step up to challenge him, The Kool Kids will!" said JoJo.

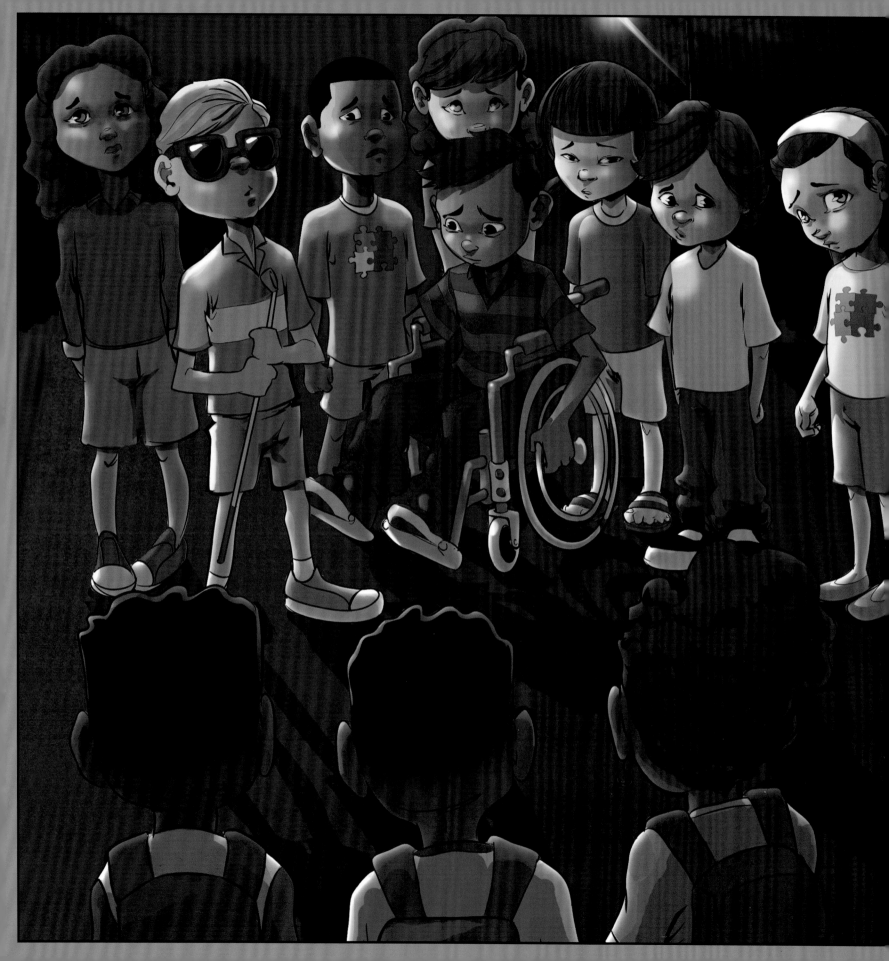

On their journey they ran into some of their friends who looked sad.

"What's wrong?" asked Jen.

"Are you guys ok?" asked Jax.

"Obesity has captured my parents," replied one friend.

"Obesity has captured my grandparents," said another friend.

"Wow!" said JoJo. "Obesity must go!"

"Let's go," said Jen.

"Can we go, too?" asked the friends.

"Sure! Let's go!" said Jax.

On the way to find Obesity,
The Kool Kids and their friends
reached a strange looking place.

"What is this place?" asked JoJo.

"It's a food desert," replied Jax.

"What's a food desert?" asked Jen.

"A food desert is a place where people
do not have access to healthy food.
All they have close to them are fast
food places.

When you find a food desert, that
means a giant is very close," said Jax.

This made Jen very sad.

"Don't cry Jen. We'll find Obesity and
put an end to all of this," said JoJo.

The Kool Kids finally reached the area where Obesity was and he was much bigger than they had imagined. They knew a giant was big, but Obesity was HUGE!"

"Soon the entire land will be under my control!!!" roared Obesity.

"No one has attempted to challenge me yet! Is there not one brave person who will challenge me!?"

The Angels whispered, "pray and push the colored button on your crosses."

The Kids look at each other and say,

"It's time for battle!"

They each push the colored button on their cross and yell,

"God of mercy, God of might,
Please give us what we need,
To win this fight!"

"Not one, but you have THREE challengers!!!" the kids say in unison.

"AND WHO ARE YOU!?" yelled Obesity.

"WE ARE THE KOOL KIDS!" replied Jax, JoJo & Jen.

"HA HA HA!!!!" Obesity laughed. "OUT OF EVERYONE IN THIS LAND, I GET CHALLENGED BY 3 PUNY KIDS?!

YOU CANNOT BE SERIOUS!"

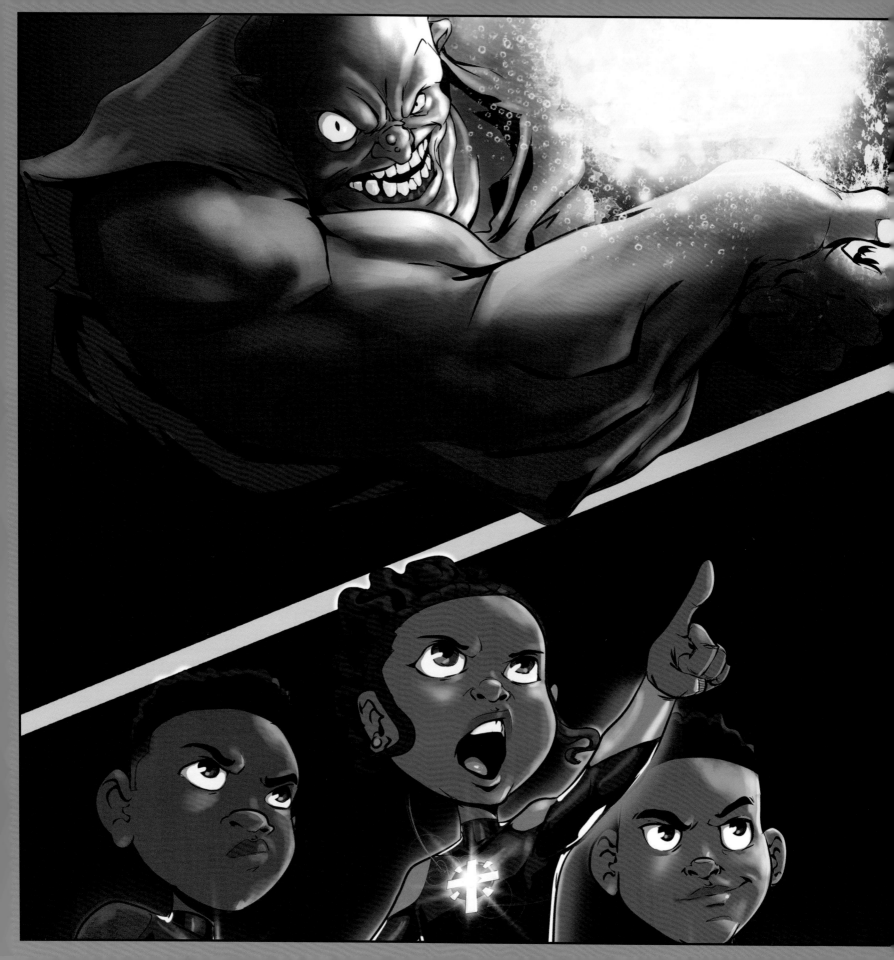

DO YOU NOT REALIZE
WHO I AM!? I AM OBESITY!
I HAVE DESTROYED MORE
LIVES IN LANDS NEAR AND
FAR! YOU HAVE TO
BRING MORE THAN 3
KIDS TO STOP ME!"

"We aren't just any 3 kids!" said Jen.

"We are the Kool Kids!" said Jax.

"And we have God on our side
and we know how to beat
you!" said JoJo.

Obesity became upset and started
to throw a huge ball of fattening
foods and sugary drinks at the Kids.
Jen saw the foods and drinks
coming and jumped in front of
Jax and JoJo. Jen's cross
lit up and a large shield projected
out of it to protect them from
Obesity's attack.

"Thanks for being alert Jen!" said Jax.

"Jesus really protected us right when
we needed Him," said JoJo.

The crosses started to blink, and slingshots projected out of them.

"Slingshots! Just like King David," said the Kids with excitement.

The kids noticed stones by their feet. They put them in their slingshots. Once the stones were in the slingshots, they turned into healthy fruits and vegetables. They fired the food at Obesity and he screamed,

"I HATE FRUIT!!!
"I HATE VEGGIES!!!!"

Jen's cross begins to blink. Her shoes have turned into skates.

Jax turns to Jen.

"Jen, use those Kool skates to make him move. Remember, Obesity hates exercise."

"Will do!" says Jen.

Jen circles around Obesity, forcing him to move.

"STOP MOVING!!! I HATE EXERCISE!!!" screamed Obesity.

Every stone that Jen put into her slingshot turns into a water bottle.

"I HATE WATER!!!" cried Obesity.

Obesity tries to throw greasy foods and sweets at The Kool Kids, but he is too tired and weak to do so. Their friends watch in amazement as The Kool Kids fight Obesity as a team.

Obesity is very weak from being hit by the healthy foods, exercise, and water and decides to retreat.

"THIS WILL NOT BE THE LAST YOU SEE OF ME KOOL KIDS!!" screamed Obesity.

"I'll BE BACK AND I WILL BRING MY FRIENDS WITH ME NEXT TIME!!!"

The shadow that covered The Land is
now gone and the people are no longer
imprisoned by Obesity. Everyone
is cheering for the Kool Kids.

Their friends surround them and say,
"THAT WAS SO KOOL!!!"

Thanks to the Kool Kids, we now know
how to defeat Obesity, and we'll share
those 8 steps with our families and friends
in the other lands to help them just in case Obesity tries
to attack them.

But please, tell us, "HOW CAN WE
BECOME KOOL KIDS AND GET
CROSSES LIKE THAT!?"

The Kids look at each other and
then turn to their friends and say,

"Sit down. Let us tell you about
our friend Jesus...."

About the Author

James Tate's personal journey to lose weight and keep it off, resulted in him establishing Beyond W8 Loss Total Wellness Center LLC, a Christ-led "Wholelistic" wellness center focused on "Total Fat Loss" (Mental, Spiritual, Emotional, Physical) and improving overall health. He uses his experience as a certified Integrative Nutrition Health Coach, Nutrition Therapist, Clinical Weight Loss Practitioner, and Sports & Exercise Nutritional Advisor to help people reach their wellness goals. Additionally, Tate is certified as a health minister through Wesley Theological Seminary.

Growing up in Washington, D.C., Tate was always a big child, a big teenager and a big adult. Tate's lowest high school weight was 275 pounds. In 2010, he weighed 415 pounds which forced him to begin his wellness journey. By January 2011, he had shed 200-plus pounds without any surgery, shots, pills or fad diets.

Tate is also the founder of The Holy & Healthy Ministry, which has several programs including: The Fight 4 Your Life, Knocking Out Obesity & Disease Movement. He uses boxing as an analogy to show people that their battles are winnable. Another program, Temple Renovation, is a wellness program that helps people "renovate" different areas of their body and life with the help of "The Master Carpenter," who is Jesus.

A graduate of the Institute for Integrative Nutrition, Tate is trained in more than 100 dietary theories. He studied a variety of practical lifestyle coaching methods. He also was trained at The Health Sciences Academy, where he earned certifications in Nutrition Therapy, as a Sports & Exercise Nutritional Advisor, and as a Clinical Weight Loss Practitioner. Drawing on this knowledge, Tate is able to help people create a completely personalized "roadmap to health" that suits their unique body, lifestyle, preferences and goals.

Tate is a ministry leader at the First Baptist Church of Glenarden in Landover, MD where John K. Jenkins Sr. is the Pastor.

Tate is a devoted husband and father.